SCHOOL DAYS

A Record Book from Preschool to Sixth Grade

Artwork by Julie Berg

This record book belongs to _____

...and introducing some of your very own Bug friends (clap, clap, clap)..........

ROXY

BOOKER

CHLOE

SAM

HAPPY

SPINDLES

FLUTTER

BEA

and I'm
SPEEDY
for obvious reasons

Contents...

Contents

This is a Story About Me!

My name is _____

and people like to call me _____ (it's my nickname!)

I was born on this day _____

in this city & state _____

I love the color of my hair! It's _____

and my eyes are _____

Here are some of my characteristics that I think make me special _____

_____

My mother's name is _____

I'm like my Mom in these ways _____

_____

My father's name is _____

and I'm like my Dad when I... _____

_____

Here are some
photos that I like!

PRE

This is my school: _____

My teacher's name is _____

Some of my favorite things about my teacher are _____

The first day of school was fun because _____

_____

Did you know that I love to do these school activities? _____

_____

I really like singing these songs: _____

SCHOOL

Wow! I'm so proud of myself because now I can _____

_____

_____

A lot of special events happened this year. My favorite ones were _____

_____

_____

_____

Snack time! I love to eat _____

_____

_____

When it's time to play outside, I like to _____

_____

And when it's playtime inside, it's fun to _____

_____

Me & My Special Friends

Here are the names of some of my school friends:

_____

_____

_____

_____

_____

_____

_____

We love to play together! Here are some of the things we do:

_____

_____

_____

_____

_____

My Favorite Preschool Photos

I am growing! I weigh this much: _____

and I am this tall: _____

Holidays and Parties

Halloween

I dressed up as... _____

_____

Where we trick-or-treated: _____

_____

Winter Holidays

I celebrated by _____

_____

Valentine's Day

The best cards were: _____

_____

_____

I had fun because _____

_____

Easter

The best egg hunt: _____

The best egg I colored: _____

Birthdays

My favorite birthday gift: _____

_____

Fun birthday parties this year: ___

_____

_____

_____

It's Summertime!

These are the places where we vacationed this year: _____

_____

_____

_____

Here are some of my favorite summer trips: _____

_____

_____

And here is a list of some of my summer friends' names: _____

_____

_____

About This Year

Here is something I will remember about my school year _____

_____

_____

_____

_____

I had so much fun in school this year because _____

_____

_____

_____

_____

When I grow up, I want to be: _____

Because _____

keepsakes & photos

Here is a picture I drew

This is my school: _____

My teacher's name is _____

Some of my favorite things about my teacher are _____

_____

_____

The first day of school was fun because _____

_____

_____

Did you know that I love to do these school activities? _____

_____

I have some favorite subjects! They are: _____

_____

I really like singing these songs: _____

And these are the toys I play with: _____

_____

Wow! I'm so proud of myself because now I can _____

_____

_____

A lot of special events happened this year. My favorite ones were _____

_____

_____

I really like it when I get this for lunch _____

_____

Snack time! I love to eat _____

_____

When it's time to play, I like to _____

_____

_____

Special Friends

Here are the names of some of my school friends:

_____

_____

_____

_____

_____

We love to play together! Here are
some of the things we do:

_____

_____

_____

These Photos
are Special!

I'm getting bigger! This year I weigh:_____and I am _____tall!

School Year Holidays

Halloween

I dressed up as... _____

_____

Where we trick-or-treated: _____

_____

Winter Holidays

I celebrated by _____

_____

Valentine's Day

The best cards were: _____

_____

I had fun because _____

_____

Easter

The best egg hunt: _____

The best egg I colored looked like

_____

Birthdays

My favorite birthday gift:

_____

Fun birthday parties this year:

_____

_____

_____

Here are some of my special summer friends:

_____

_____

_____

_____

_____

Summertime Fun

And we did a lot of fun things like: _____

_____

_____

A special time spent with my family was when we... _____

_____

Here are some of my favorite summer trips: _____

_____

About This Year

Here is something I will remember about my school year _____

_____

_____

_____

I had so much fun in school this year because _____

_____

_____

_____

When I grow up, I want to be: _____

Because _____

Here is a
picture I drew

This is my school: _____

My teacher's name is _____

Some of my favorite things about my teacher are _____

_____

_____

The first day of school was fun because _____

_____

_____

Did you know that I love to do these school activities? _____

_____

I have some favorite subjects! They are: _____

_____

I really like singing these songs: _____

And these are the toys I play with: _____

Wow! I'm so proud of myself because now I can _____

_____

A lot of special events happened this year. My favorite ones were _____

_____

_____

_____

_____

I really like it when I get this for lunch _____

_____

Snack time! I love to eat _____

When it's time to play, I like to _____

_____

_____

Special Friends

Here are the names of some of my school friends:

_____

_____

_____

_____

_____

_____

_____

_____

We love to play together! Here are

some of the things we do:

These Photos
are Special to me!

Don't I grow fast! I weigh this much: _____ and I am this tall: _____

School Year Holidays

Halloween

I dressed up as... _____

_____

Where we trick-or-treated: _____

_____

Winter Holidays

I celebrated by _____

_____

Valentine's Day

The best cards were:

_____

I had fun because _____

_____

Easter

The best egg hunt: _____

The best egg I colored looked like _____

_____

Birthdays

My favorite birthday gift: _____

_____

Fun birthday parties this year:

_____

_____

_____

_____

It's Summertime!

Here are some of my special summer friends _____

_____

And we did a lot of fun things like: _____

_____

_____

A special time spent with my family was when we... _____

_____

_____

Here are some of my favorite summer trips: _____

_____

_____

_____

About This Year

Here is something I will remember about my school year _____

_____

_____

_____

_____

I had so much fun in school this year because _____

_____

_____

_____

When I grow up, I want to be: _____

Because _____

keepsakes & photos

Here is a picture I drew

This is my school: _____

My teacher's name is _____

Some of my favorite things about my teacher are _____

_____

_____

The first day of school was fun because _____

_____

_____

Did you know that I love to do these school activities? _____

_____

I have some favorite subjects! They are: _____

_____

I really like singing these songs: _____

And these are the toys I play with: _____

Wow! I'm so proud of myself because now I can _____

_____

_____

A lot of special events happened this year. My favorite ones were _____

_____

_____

_____

I really like it when I get this for lunch _____

_____

Snack time! I love to eat _____

_____

When it's time to play, I like to _____

_____

_____

Here are the names of some of my school friends: _____

_____

_____

_____

Special Friends

We love to play together! Here are some of the things we do: _____

_____

_____

These are Special 3rd Grade Photos!

I'm growing all the time! Can you believe I weigh _____ and I am _____ tall?!

School Year Holidays

Halloween

I dressed up as... _____

Where we trick-or-treated: _____

Winter Holidays

I celebrated by _____

Valentine's Day

The best cards were: _____

I had fun because _____

Easter

The best egg hunt: _____

The best egg I colored looked like _____

_____

Birthdays

My favorite birthday gift: _____

Fun birthday parties this year: _____

_____

Summertime Fun!

Here are some of my special summer friends _____

_____

And we did a lot of fun things like: _____

_____

_____

A special time spent with my family was when we... _____

_____

_____

Here are some of my favorite summer trips: _____

_____

_____

About This Year

Here is something I will remember about my school year _____

_____

_____

_____

I had so much fun in school this year because _____

_____

_____

_____

When I grow up, I want to be: _____

Because _____

Here is a picture I drew

This is my school: _____

My teacher's name is _____

Some of my favorite things about my teacher are _____

_____

_____

The first day of school was fun because _____

_____

_____

Did you know that I love to do these school activities? _____

_____

I have some favorite subjects! They are: _____

_____

I really like singing these songs: _____

And these are the toys I play with: _____

Wow! I'm so proud of myself because now I can _____

_____

_____

_____

A lot of special events happened this year. My favorite ones were _____

_____

_____

I really like it when I get this for lunch: _____

_____

Snack time! I love to eat _____

When it's time to play, I like to _____

_____

_____

Special Friends

Here are the names of some of my school friends:

_____

_____

_____

_____

We love to play together! Here are

some of the things we do:

_____

_____

_____

_____

_____

Here are some
really Special Photos!

School Year Holidays

Halloween

I dressed up as... _____

_____

Where we trick-or-treated: _____

_____

Winter Holidays

I celebrated by _____

_____

_____

Valentine's Day

The best cards were: _____

_____

I had fun because _____

_____

Easter

The best egg hunt: _____

The best egg I colored looked like:

_____

Birthdays

My favorite birthday gift: _____

Fun birthday parties this year: _____

_____

It's Summertime!

Here are some of my special summer friends _____

_____

And we did a lot of fun things like: _____

_____

A special time spent with my family was when we... _____

_____

_____

Here are some of my favorite summer trips: _____

_____

_____

_____

About This Year

Here is something I will remember about my school year _____

_____

_____

_____

I had so much fun in school this year because _____

_____

I received some awards this year! They are _____

_____

When I grow up, I want to be: _____

_____

Because _____

Here is a picture I drew...

This is my school: _____

My teacher's name is _____

Some of my favorite things about my teacher are _____

_____

_____

The first day of school was fun because _____

_____

_____

Did you know that I love to do these school activities? _____

_____

I have some favorite subjects! They are: _____

_____

Some fun school activities are: _____

_____

Wow! I'm so proud of myself because now I can _____

_____

_____

My favorite events that happened this year are _____

_____

At lunch I just love to eat: _____

_____

Snack time! I love to eat _____

_____

Some of my favorite activities are: _____

_____

_____

_____

The sports I play and the clubs I am in are: _____

_____

_____

_____

Special Friends

Here are the names of some of my school friends:

_____

_____

_____

_____

_____

_____

We love to play together! Here are
some of the things we do:

_____

_____

_____

_____

These are Special 5th Grade Photos!

Watch me grow! Now I weigh this much: _____

and I am this tall: _____

School Year Holidays

Halloween

I dressed up as... _____

_____

Where we trick-or-treated: _____

_____

Winter Holidays

I celebrated by _____

_____

Valentine's Day

The best cards were:

_____

I had fun because _____

_____

Easter

The best egg hunt: _____

The best egg I colored looked like ____

_____

Birthdays

My favorite birthday gift:

_____

Fun birthday parties this year:

_____

_____

_____

Summertime Fun !

Here are some of my special summer friends _____

_____

And we did a lot of fun things like: _____

_____

_____

A special time spent with my family was when we... _____

_____

_____

Here are some of my favorite summer trips: _____

_____

_____

Here is something I will remember about my school year _____

_____

I had so much fun in school this year because _____

_____

I received some awards this year! They are _____

_____

When I grow up, I want to be: _____

Because _____

About This Year

keepsakes
& photos

6th

This is my school: _____

My teacher's name is _____

Some of my favorite things about my teacher are _____

_____

_____

The first day of school was fun because _____

_____

_____

Did you know that I love to do these school activities? _____

_____

I have some favorite subjects! They are: _____

_____

Some fun school activities are: _____

_____

My favorite events that happened this year are _____

_____

At lunch I just love to eat: _____

_____

My favorite snacks are _____

Some of my favorite activities are: _____

_____

_____

The sports I play and the clubs I am in are: _____

_____

_____

I'm so proud because I've learned how to _____

_____

Special Friends

Here are the names of some of my school friends:

_____

_____

_____

_____

_____

_____

_____

We love to play together! Here are some of the things we do:

_____

_____

_____

_____

_____

Here are some
really Special Photos!

School Year Holidays

Halloween

I dressed up as... _____

Where we trick-or-treated: _____

Winter Holidays

I celebrated by _____

Valentine's Day

The best cards were: _____

I had fun because _____

Easter

The best egg hunt: _____

The best egg I colored looked like _____

_____

Birthdays

My favorite birthday gift:

_____

Fun birthday parties this year:

_____

_____

_____

_____

It's Summertime!

Here are some of my special summer friends _____

_____

And we did a lot of fun things like: _____

_____

_____

A special time spent with my family was when we... _____

_____

_____

Here are some of my favorite summer trips: _____

_____

_____

Hey...let's go!!

OK!

Me & My Future...

This is what I want to be when I grow up, and why: _____

_____

_____

_____

_____

I have learned so much! This is what I learned about myself: _____

_____

_____

_____

_____

A Letter to Me
From Mom & Dad

_____

_____

_____

_____

_____

_____

_____

_____

_____

Available Record Books from Havoc

A Celebration of Memories	Grandparents
A Circle of Love	Heart to Heart
Baby	It's All About Me!
College Life	Mom
Couples	Mothers & Daughters
Family	My Pregnancy
Forever Friends	Our Honeymoon
Generations	School Days
Girlfriends	Sisters
Grandmother	Tying the Knot

Havoc
PUBLISHING

Please write to us with your ideas for
additional Havoc Publishing products

Havoc Publishing
9808 Waples Street
San Diego, CA 92121